Awesome Oceans

Written by Sarah O'Neil
Series Consultant: Linda Hoyt

WorldWise
Content-based Learning

Contents

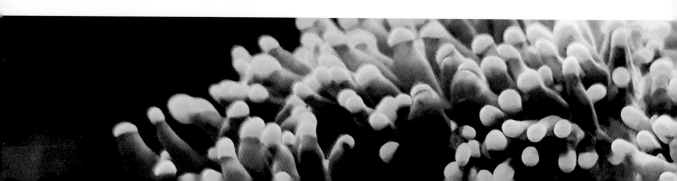

Chapter 1

Awesome oceans

Oceans are vital to all life on Earth and yet they are places of great mystery. The salty waters of the ocean cover about 70 per cent of the earth. But more people have been to the top of Mount Everest than to the deepest parts of the ocean.

Did you know?

The ocean is sometimes called the blue, the deep, Davy Jones's locker, the drink, blue water or the seven seas.

Often the surface of the ocean is calm, but at other times wind and tides push and pull the water, causing enormous waves to form. When its awesome power is unleashed, the ocean can smash ships and flood the land.

Sometimes earthquakes on the ocean floor cause huge walls of water called **tsunami**. Tsunamis can flood the land, causing greater destruction than ordinary storms.

The ocean's power is both awesome and destructive.

Ocean facts

Most of the ocean is a vast expanse of water called the open ocean. The bottom, or floor, of the open ocean is more than three kilometres deep. Many types of **terrain**, such as plains and mountains, are found here. Mount Everest may be the highest mountain on land, but higher mountains are found rising from the floor in the open ocean. The deepest **trenches** on Earth are also found in the ocean. In these trenches the water may be as deep as 11 kilometres.

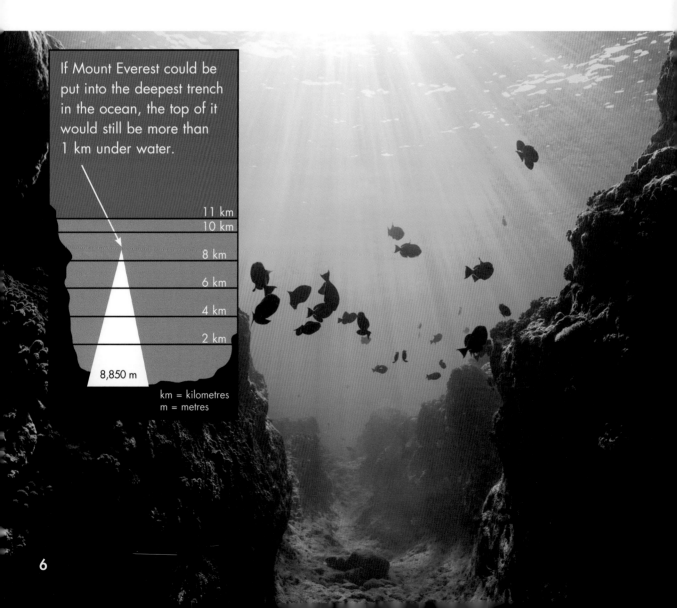

If Mount Everest could be put into the deepest trench in the ocean, the top of it would still be more than 1 km under water.

11 km
10 km
8 km
6 km
4 km
2 km
8,850 m

km = kilometres
m = metres

There are five oceans: the **Atlantic, Pacific, Indian, Arctic** and **Southern.**

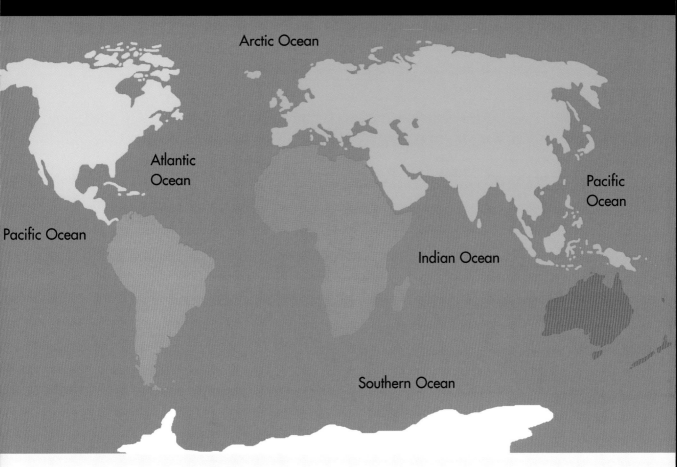

Arctic Ocean

Atlantic Ocean

Pacific Ocean

Pacific Ocean

Indian Ocean

Southern Ocean

Size and depth of the oceans

Ocean	Area (km²)	Deepest depth (m²)
Pacific	155,557,000	Mariana Trench 10,924
Atlantic	76,762,000	Puerto Rico Trench 8,605
Indian	68,556,000	Java Trench 7,258
Southern	20,327,000	South Sandwich Trench 7,235
Arctic	14,056,000	Fram Basin 4,665
km² = square kilometres m = metres		

Chapter 2

Ocean life

Living in the open ocean

Most **marine** animals swim in the top 200 metres of the open ocean. This water is the warmest in the open ocean because sunlight can penetrate it. As the water gets deeper less light penetrates and it becomes steadily colder and darker. In the deepest oceans, the temperature is as low as 1 degree Celsius.

Water pressure also increases greatly as the ocean gets deeper. In the deepest part of the ocean, water pressure is 100 times greater than at the surface. Water pressure is caused by the weight of the water above pressing down on the ocean floor and the animals that live there.

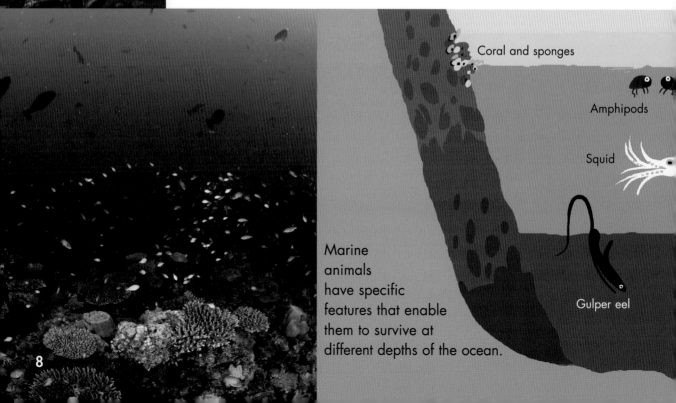

Coral and sponges

Amphipods

Squid

Gulper eel

Marine animals have specific features that enable them to survive at different depths of the ocean.

Animals that live near the surface cannot live in the deeper water because it is too dark and too cold for them to survive there. The water pressure would crush them, they could not see to find food and they would get too cold.

But some animals do live in the ocean's depths. Their bodies are suited to the deep, dark environment. They need the cold temperatures, the darkness and the immense water pressure of the deep water to survive.

You will need:
- a bucket full of water
- a drinking straw
- a large plastic bag

What to do
1. Use the straw to blow bubbles at different depths in the water in the bucket. Notice what happens to the bubbles as the bottom of the straw gets deeper into the water. This is caused by water pressure.

2. Put your hand and arm inside the plastic bag. Slowly lower your hand into the bucket. What do you feel as your hand goes deeper into the bucket? This is water pressure.

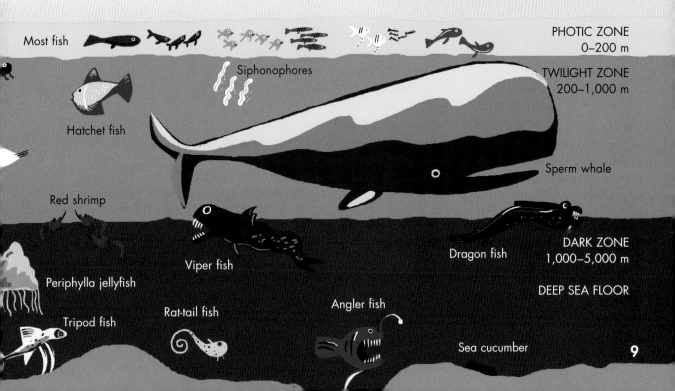

Most fish

Siphonophores

Hatchet fish

Red shrimp

Viper fish

Periphylla jellyfish

Tripod fish

Rat-tail fish

Angler fish

Dragon fish

Sperm whale

Sea cucumber

PHOTIC ZONE
0–200 m

TWILIGHT ZONE
200–1,000 m

DARK ZONE
1,000–5,000 m

DEEP SEA FLOOR

Living at the edge of the ocean

Coastal waters are areas of ocean near land. The water here is much shallower than the water in the open ocean. Coastal waters are always changing because of the wind, waves and tides. Many marine animals that live close to the shore must be able to survive changes in the water depth as the tides come in and go out.

In coastal waters, sunlight can reach the floor of the ocean, so seagrasses and seaweeds are able to grow there. Many animals use seagrass meadows or kelp forests for food and shelter. This makes coastal areas a good place for land and sea animals to find food.

Some animals visit coastal waters to breed. Others, such as sea turtles, come to lay their eggs on the beach. But storms and the movement of the tides make coastal waters difficult places to live in, so many animals visit this part of the ocean only when they have to.

▲ Manatees are large mammals that live in coastal waters near the southern United States, Central and South America, and some seas of east Africa. They are related to dugongs, which live near northern Australia.

▶
▼ Animals that live in coastal waters may remain out of the water when the tide is low. They are able to stop their bodies from drying out during this time. Some have hard shells that help keep them moist.

Living together

Some living things have a special relationship with each other and help each other to stay alive and healthy. Such a relationship is called a **symbiotic relationship**. Symbiotic means living together. Symbiotic relationships may involve animals cleaning, feeding, protecting or sheltering each other.

Anemones and clown fish have a symbiotic relationship. Anemones have poisonous tentacles that kill most fish. But clown fish are **immune** to anemones' poison. Clown fish clean anemones and attract fish that anemones can eat. In return, anemones' tentacles protect clown fish from **predators**. The clown fish can also eat food that anemones leave.

▼ Clown fish swim in the anemone's tentacles without being hurt.

Some small fish can live among the stinging tentacles of some jellyfish. They are immune to the sting. The fish keep the jellyfish clean, and may attract bigger fish for the jellyfish to eat. The small fish are kept safe by the jellyfish.

Cleaner fish get food by scraping clean coral trout's skin. Coral trout eat other fish, but they don't eat cleaner fish because coral trout need clean skin.

▲ This jellyfish has small fish living among its tentacles.

▼ Cleaner fish nibble a coral trout clean.

13

Chapter 3

What do sea animals eat?

What's for dinner?

Most animals depend on other living things for food.   Some eat plants, and some hunt other animals or eat the bodies of dead animals. In the food web on the next page we can see how animals that live in or near the sea rely on other living things for their survival.

Food web

means "is eaten by"
or "are eaten by"

tiny plants

seaweed

mussels

sea snail

limpets

sea star

tiny animals

crab

seagull

fish

seal

Hunting for food

Many animals that live in the sea eat other animals. These **predators** have many different ways of catching their food.

Nice smile
Animal: Great white shark
Diet: Fish, seals
Hunting technique: Great white sharks have many rows of razor-sharp teeth that they use to catch other animals. These teeth point backwards, which makes it very difficult for an animal to escape once it has been bitten.

It's a great strain
Animal: Blue whale
Diet: Plankton
Hunting technique: Blue whales do not have teeth. Instead, they have huge **baleen** plates that they use to filter tiny ocean plants and animals from the water.

Sounds great
Animal: Bottlenose dolphin
Diet: Fish
Hunting technique: Bottlenose dolphins, like other dolphins, use sound to find food. Dolphins hunt in groups. They find their prey and herd it towards the surface of the water where it is easier to catch.

Avoiding predators

It is difficult for animals that live in the open ocean to avoid predators because there are not many places to hide. Some **marine** animals **camouflage** themselves. Some fish are coloured in a way that makes them difficult to see. They are dark on top and light underneath. This hides them because their light undersides blend in with the light surface of the ocean when seen from below, and their dark tops are difficult to distinguish from the dark depths of the ocean when seen from above.

Safety in numbers
Animal: Bluefin tuna
Diet: Small fish
Hunting technique:
Bluefin tuna are able to keep their bodies warm, which enables them to swim faster than their prey. Bluefin tuna hunt in **schools**, driving other fish towards the surface, where they are easier to catch.

What's your poison?
Animal: Box jellyfish
Diet: Small fish
Hunting technique:
Box jellyfish trail very long poisonous tentacles behind them as they drift through the water. Any animal that touches these tentacles is paralysed by the jellyfish's poison. Then the jellyfish can eat it.

Am I boring you?
Animal: Sea snail
Diet: Shellfish
Hunting technique:
Sea snails crawl onto the shell of another shellfish and use their drill-like tongue to make a hole in the shell. Then they eat the animal through the hole.

Some animals swim in large groups called schools to protect themselves. It is much harder for a predator to catch an animal that is part of a large group.

▶ These fish swim close together in circles to try to confuse predators.

17

Chapter 4

Exploring the ocean

The role of technology

Exploring the deepest parts of the ocean is difficult and dangerous. Humans cannot survive the cold and the **water pressure** at the bottom of the ocean without the protection of specially built **submersibles**. These underwater boats have very strong bodies and thick windows, as well as powerful lights so the scientists in them can see in the darkness. The **bathysphere** is one kind of submersible. Scientists in submersibles can catch **marine** animals in nets and make video and sound recordings of the ocean floor so they can learn more about life there.

▼ Unprotected, humans can dive only to relatively shallow depths.

Using the bathysphere

crane

steel cable

companion vessel

air hose

the bathysphere

lights

access hatch

Dr Beebe's bathysphere was the first manned deep-sea submersible.

Timeline of development of deep-sea exploration technology

1876 The first deep-sea fish is found, using a net.

1930 The first deep-sea submersible, the bathysphere, could travel to 805 metres. It was built by Otis Barton and Dr William Beebe.

1948 Auguste Piccard designed and built a **bathyscaphe** that could dive to 4,000 metres.

1960 Don Walsh and Jacques Piccard made a record dive in the bathyscaphe *Trieste* to about 11,000 metres in the Challenger Deep.

1964 The first maneuverable deep-sea submersible was built. This could not only dive but also move around the ocean floor.

2012 James Cameron dived in the submersible *Deepsea Challenger* to the bottom of the Challenger Deep. He reached a record depth for a solo dive of about 11,000 metres.

Meet an oceanographer

My name is Charlie. I am a deep-sea **oceanographer**. I study the animals that live in the deepest parts of the ocean. To do this, I travel to the bottom of the ocean in a small submersible that has been specially designed to withstand the enormous water pressure there.

My submersible has a lot of equipment to help me do my research. It has strong lights so I can see where I am going in the total darkness at the bottom of the ocean. It has cameras and microphones so I can record any animals I see. It also has nets that I can use to catch any animals I want to study further when I get back to the surface.

I feel like an explorer as I move around the ocean floor. I get to see things that very few people have ever seen. Last month I discovered an animal that no one knew existed. My job is very exciting.

◄ The submersible can take rock samples from the ocean floor.

Deep-sea fish like those below are seldom seen because it is difficult for people to travel into the deep. More people have been into space than to the very deepest parts of the ocean.

▼ This fish glows in the dark to attract prey.

▼ The angler fish attracts food by lighting up a lure on the end of its fin.

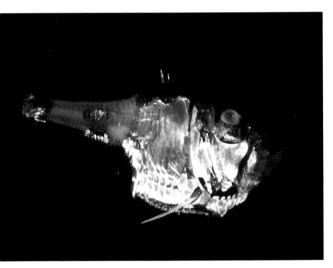

◄ A viper fish has long sharp teeth. These help it to hold on to any food it catches.

Chapter 5

Feeding people from the ocean

Fishing

Millions of tonnes of fish are caught all around the world each year. Most fish are caught by professional fisherpeople who sell them for food. People around the world depend on fish from the oceans for food. For thousands of years, people assumed that the oceans would provide an unlimited amount of food. Today, we know that this is not true. Many animals have been overfished and now are endangered. Overfishing occurs when so many fish are caught that there are not enough fish left in the ocean to reproduce and to keep numbers constant.

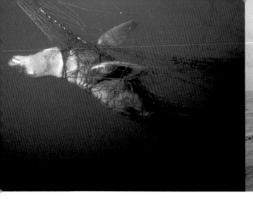

Thousands of kilometres of nets and lines are used in the world's oceans to catch fish each day. These nets and lines catch other **marine** animals such as dolphins and turtles that are not being fished. Animals that are not meant to be caught are called bycatch. Around 40 per cent of the world's fishing catch is bycatch. Bycatch are usually thrown back into the ocean, but they do not usually survive. Many of these marine animals are endangered.

Trawling boats drag large nets along the seabed, catching almost everything in their path. They can damage coral reefs and catch marine turtles.

Longlining is a **commercial fishing** method where hundreds or thousands of baited hooks hang along a fishing line. Marine turtles and sharks often swallow these hooks and die.

▼ This shark was caught in a bycatch. It was returned to the ocean.

Chapter 6

Looking after the ocean

Marine parks

The governments of many countries have created protected **marine** areas like the ones shown on the map on the right because fishing is so popular. Protected marine areas are ocean **habitats** where people are not allowed to cause any damage. In these areas there are rules about what people can and cannot do. Anyone who breaks these rules can be **prosecuted**.

What you can do
Snorkelling
Scuba diving
Sailing and boating
Educational excursions
Scientific research

What you cannot do
Recreational or **commercial fishing**
Oil and mining exploration
Anything that harms the protected area

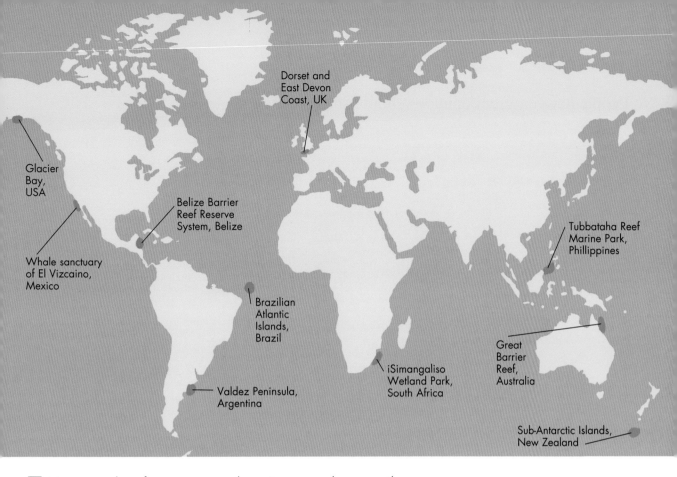

Dorset and
East Devon
Coast, UK

Glacier
Bay,
USA

Belize Barrier
Reef Reserve
System, Belize

Whale sanctuary
of El Vizcaino,
Mexico

Tubbataha Reef
Marine Park,
Phillippines

Brazilian
Atlantic
Islands,
Brazil

Great
Barrier
Reef,
Australia

iSimangaliso
Wetland Park,
South Africa

Valdez Peninsula,
Argentina

Sub-Antarctic Islands,
New Zealand

▼ Many coral reefs are protected marine areas because they
are places that support a huge number of sea animals.

What's your opinion?

People have different opinions about protected marine areas.

Some people say:

There are plenty of fish in the ocean, so there is nothing to worry about.

Fisherpeople will be unemployed if they are not allowed to catch fish wherever the fish are found.

People should be able to catch fish anywhere in the ocean because people need to eat. Fish is a healthy food for people.

Other people say:

There are fewer fish in the ocean than there used to be.

Because many of the fish in the ocean are endangered, we need to give them safe places to live and breed or they will disappear forever.

Fisherpeople will have no jobs if there are no fish left to catch.

What do you think?

World Oceans Day

SANDY COVE CLEANUP

8 June Beach lovers in Sandy Cove were out in force today, armed with garbage bags and rubber gloves. They were celebrating World Oceans Day by cleaning up the dunes and rock pools in the town's popular bay.

This year the annual event attracted a record number of participants. Lifesaver Andrew Jones said, "I'm thrilled that so many people came along and helped today. Lots of little children come to the beach and they need a clean and safe place to swim and play."

The local diving club spent the day cleaning up Sandpipers Reef. "We found plastic bags, bits of fishing nets and fishing line, rusty hooks and other rubbish. These things can kill the local sea turtles and seabirds. I'm glad the rubbish is gone," said Zeinab Akmed, president of the Sandy Cove Dive Club.

Town mayor, Claire Onski, congratulated everyone on an excellent effort. "From now on we should act as if every day is World Oceans Day," she said.

Think about ...

What could you do to support the next World Oceans Day?

World Oceans Day was first declared in 1992 at the **Earth Summit**, which was held in Rio de Janeiro, Brazil. World Oceans Day is celebrated on 8 June each year. This day was created because those who attended the Earth Summit were concerned about the damage being done to the world's oceans. They wanted people to think about this problem and to take better care of oceans.

Glossary

baleen
long strands of stiff hair in the mouths of baleen whales used to sift food from the water

bathyscaphe
a deep-sea diving submersible that, unlike the bathysphere, can propel itself

bathysphere
a submersible that can be lowered deep into the ocean

camouflage
to use colour or covering to look like the surroundings

commercial fishing
catching fish and other sea animals to sell

Earth Summit
the United Nations international conference on environment and development

habitat
a place where a plant or animal naturally lives

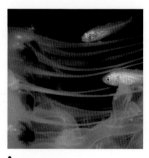

immune
not affected by poison or disease

marine
things that are found in or relate to the sea

oceanographer
scientist who studies and works in the ocean

predators
animals that kill and eat other animals

prosecute
take to court for breaking the law

recreational fishing
fishing for fun, not money

school
a large number of the same kind of fish that swim together

submersible
a boat that travels underwater

symbiotic relationship
living together for shelter, food, cleaning or protection

terrain
physical features of the land – hardness, slope, surface and so on

trench
a deep, narrow cut in the land or seabed

tsunami
a huge wave caused by an underwater volcano, earthquake or landslide

water pressure
the strength at which water presses on an object, increasing with the depth of the water

Index